DRAGONS
Coloring Book for Kids

This Book belongs to:

Ages:

Copyright © 2023 Penelope Moore . All Rights Reserved.

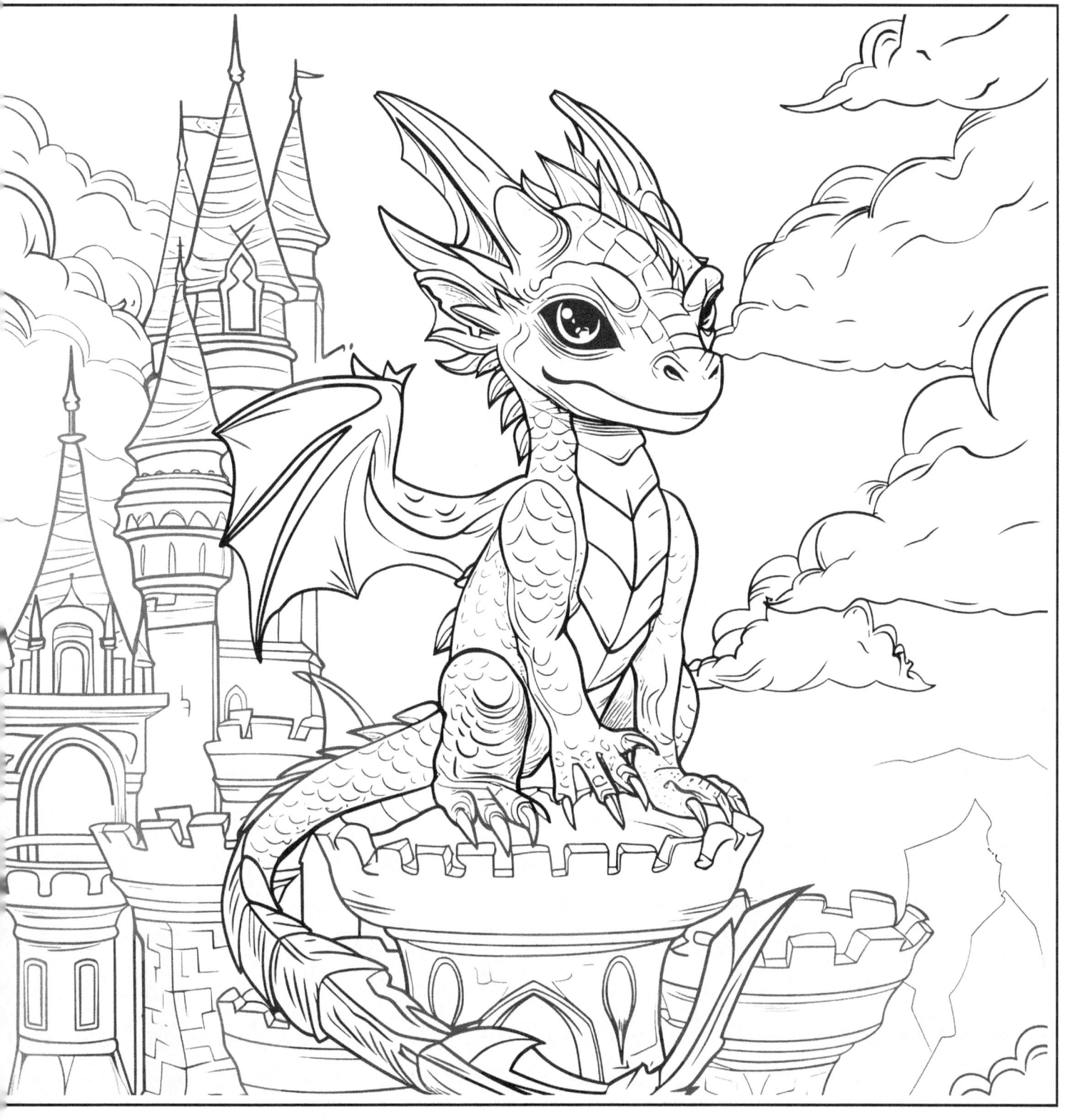

Congratulations, little dragon artists! You've journeyed through a magical world of colors and creativity, bringing adorable baby dragons to life with your imagination. As you close this book, remember that the power to create and dream is always within you. Keep coloring your world with joy, laughter, and endless possibilities. Until we meet again, may your days be filled with adventure and your dreams take flight like a dragon's gentle soar. Farewell, and keep spreading your wings!

www.ingramcontent.com/pod-product-compliance
Lightning Source LLC
Chambersburg PA
CBHW082210070526
44585CB00020B/2363